WHAT'S COOKING?

ITALIAN

PARRAGON

First published in Great Britain in 1997 by
Parragon
Unit 13–17
Avonbridge Trading Estate
Atlantic Road
Avonmouth
Bristol BS11 9QD

ISBN: 0-7525-2256-6

Produced by Haldane Mason, London

Acknowledgements
Art Director: Ron Samuels
Designer: Zoë Mellors
Editors: Jo-Anne Cox, Charles Dixon-Spain
Photography: Karl Adamson, Martin Brigdale, Amanda Heywood

Printed in Italy

Material in this book has previously appeared in *Italian Regional Cooking* by Rosemary Wadey, *Cooking on a Budget* by Sue Ashworth and *Quick & Easy Meals* by Carole Handslip

Note

Cup measurements in this book are for American cups. Tablespoons are assumed to be 15ml. Unless otherwise stated, milk is assumed to be full fat, eggs are standard size 3 and pepper is freshly ground black pepper.

CONTENTS

Introduction

All the colour, warmth and flavour of Italian cooking are captured in this exciting and varied collection of recipes. Whether you want to cook a classic Italian dish such as Saltimbocca or try a traditional Fish Stew, this book is packed with exciting ideas for any meal, from the simplest lunch to the most sumptuous dinner.

Much of Italian cooking depends on one staple ingredient: pasta. Pasta comes in all shapes and sizes and is available both fresh and dried. Lasagne, cannelloni, penne, fettuccine and macaroni are but a few; try them all, and maybe you will find a favourite. It is often said that the larger the pasta shapes the richer the sauce should be, but that is a matter of preference. It is also said that guests should wait for the pasta to be ready and not vice versa; but as pasta does not take long to cook, that should not be a problem. Whichever pasta you prepare however, make sure it is served *al dente*, i.e. tender but still with a slight bite to it – soggy pasta is not very palatable, at least not to Italians.

Italy is divided up into many distinct culinary regions, and this book takes recipes from all of them to provide an often surprising but always delicious mixture of taste and aromas. The first recipes in this book are *antipasti* and soups like Minestrone and Crostini alla Fiorentina, followed by pastas and pizzas. Fish and seafood add a lighter texture to the next recipes, and then come meat and poultry. While Italians are famed for their love of good food and good wine, it's not often remembered that their desserts are also absolutely delicious. To prove the point, this book finishes with several very Italian – and very wicked – desserts like Ricotta Ice Cream and Tiramisu.

Fish Soup

The selection of Italian fish soups is enormous. This one, from Tuscany, is more like a chowder.

SERVES 4–6

1 kg/2 lb assorted prepared fish (including mixed fish fillets, squid, etc.)
2 onions, thinly sliced • a few sprigs of parsley
2 bay leaves • 2 celery sticks, thinly sliced
150 ml/¼ pint/⅔ cup white wine
1 litre/1¾ pints/4 cups water
2 tbsp olive oil • 1 garlic clove, crushed
1 carrot, peeled and finely chopped
425 g/14 oz can of peeled tomatoes, puréed
2 potatoes, peeled and chopped • 1 tbsp tomato purée (paste)
1 tsp freshly chopped oregano or ½ tsp dried oregano
350 g/12 oz fresh mussels
175 g/6 oz peeled prawns (shrimp)
2 tbsp freshly chopped parsley • salt and pepper
crusty bread, to serve

1 Cut the cleaned and prepared fish into slices or cubes and put into a large saucepan with 1 sliced onion, the parsley sprigs and bay leaves, 1 sliced celery stick, the wine and the water. Bring to the boil, cover and simmer for about 25 minutes.

2 Strain the fish stock and discard the vegetables. Skin the fish, remove any bones and reserve.

3 Heat the oil in a pan, finely chop the remaining onion and fry with the garlic, remaining celery and carrot until soft but not coloured. Add the puréed canned tomatoes, potatoes, tomato purée (paste), oregano, reserved stock and seasonings. Bring to the boil and simmer for about 15 minutes or until the potato is almost tender.

4 Meanwhile, thoroughly scrub the mussels. Add to the pan with the prawns (shrimp) and simmer for about 5 minutes or until the mussels have opened (discard any that remain closed).

5 Return the fish to the soup and add the chopped parsley, bring back to the boil and simmer for 5 minutes. Adjust the seasoning, if necessary.

6 Serve the soup in warmed bowls with chunks of fresh crusty bread, or put a toasted slice of crusty bread in the bottom of each bowl before adding the soup. If possible, remove a few half shells from the mussels before serving.

Minestrone with Pesto

Minestrone always contains a variety of vegetables, pasta and rice. This version also includes beans.

SERVES 6

175 g/6 oz/scant 1 cup dried cannellini beans, soaked overnight
2½ litres/4 pints/10 cups water or stock
1 large onion, chopped • 1 leek, trimmed and sliced thinly
2 celery stalks, sliced very thinly • 2 carrots, chopped
3 tbsp olive oil • 2 tomatoes, peeled and chopped roughly
1 courgette (zucchini), trimmed and sliced thinly
2 potatoes, diced
90 g/3 oz elbow macaroni, or other small macaroni
salt and pepper • 4–6 tbsp freshly grated Parmesan

Pesto:

2 tbsp pine kernels (nuts) • 5 tbsp olive oil
2 bunches basil, stems removed
4–6 garlic cloves, crushed
90 g/3 oz/1 cup Pecorino or Parmesan, grated
salt and pepper

1 Drain the beans, rinse and put in a saucepan with the water or stock. Bring to the boil, cover and simmer gently for 1 hour. Add the onion, leek, celery, carrots and oil to the pan. Cover and simmer for 4–5 minutes. Add the tomatoes, courgette (zucchini), potatoes and macaroni and season. Cover again and continue to simmer for about 30 minutes or until very tender.

2 Meanwhile, make the pesto. Fry the pine kernels (nuts) in 1 tablespoon of the oil until pale brown, then drain. Put the basil into a food processor or blender with the nuts and garlic. Process until well chopped. Alternatively, chop finely by

hand and pound with a pestle and mortar. Gradually add the oil until smooth. Turn into a bowl, add the cheese and season to taste, and mix thoroughly.

3 Stir $1\frac{1}{2}$ tablespoons of the pesto into the soup until well blended. Simmer for a further 5 minutes and adjust the seasoning, if necessary. Serve very hot, sprinkled with the cheese.

Mozzarella in Carozza

A delicious way of serving Mozzarella – the cheese stretches out into melted strings as you cut into the Carozza.

SERVES 4

200 g/7 oz Mozzarella
4 slices, Parma ham (prosciutto), about 90 g/3 oz
8 two-day-old slices of white bread, crusts removed
butter for spreading • 2–3 eggs
3 tbsp milk • vegetable oil for deep-frying
salt and pepper

Tomato & pepper sauce:
1 onion, chopped • 2 garlic cloves, crushed
3 tbsp olive oil
1 red (bell) pepper, cored, deseeded and chopped
425 g/14 oz can of peeled tomatoes
2 tbsp tomato purée (paste) • 3 tbsp water
1 tbsp lemon juice • salt and pepper
flat-leaf parsley, to garnish (optional)

1 First make the sauce: fry the onion and garlic in the oil until soft. Add the (bell) pepper and continue to cook for 2–3 minutes. Add the tomatoes, tomato purée (paste), water, lemon juice and seasoning. Bring to the boil, cover and simmer for 10–15 minutes or until tender. Cool the sauce a little, then purée or liquidize until smooth and return to a clean pan.

2 Cut the Mozzarella into 4 slices as large as possible; if using a square piece of cheese, cut into 8 slices. Trim the Parma ham (prosciutto) slices to the same size as the cheese. Lightly butter the bread and use the cheese and ham to make 4 sandwiches, pressing the edges together firmly. If liked, they may be cut in half at this stage. Cover with cling film (plastic wrap) and chill.

3 Lightly beat the eggs with the milk and seasoning in a shallow dish. Carefully dip the sandwiches in the egg mixture until well coated, and leave to soak for a few minutes, if possible.

4 Heat the oil in a large pan or deep-frier to 180°C–190°C/350°C–375°F, or until a cube of bread browns in about 30 seconds. Fry the sandwiches in batches until golden brown on both sides. Drain well on paper towels and keep warm.

5 Serve the sandwiches hot, with the reheated tomato and pepper sauce, garnished with parsley, if using.

Crostini alla Fiorentina

Serve as a starter, or simply spread on small pieces of crusty fried bread (crostini) as an appetizer with drinks.

SERVES 4

3 tbsp olive oil • 1 onion, chopped
1 celery stalk, chopped • 1 carrot, chopped
1–2 garlic cloves, crushed • 125 g/4 oz chicken livers
125 g/4 oz calf's, lamb's or pig's liver
150 ml/¼ pint/⅔ cup red wine
1 tbsp tomato purée (paste)
2 tbsp chopped fresh parsley
3–4 canned anchovy fillets, chopped finely
2 tbsp stock or water
30–45 g/1–1½ oz/2–3 tbsp butter • 1 tbsp capers
salt and pepper • small pieces of fried crusty bread, to serve
chopped parsley, to garnish

1 Heat the oil in a pan, add the onion, celery, carrot and garlic, and cook gently for 4–5 minutes or until the onion is soft, but not coloured.

2 Meanwhile, rinse and dry the chicken livers. Dry the calf's, lamb's or pig's liver, and slice into strips. Add the liver to the pan and fry gently for a few minutes until the strips are well sealed on all sides.

3 Add half the wine and cook until mostly evaporated. Then add the rest of the wine, tomato purée (paste), half the parsley, the anchovy fillets, stock or water, a little salt and plenty of black pepper. Cover the pan and simmer for 15–20 minutes or until tender and most of the liquid has been absorbed. Let the mixture cool a little, then either coarsely mince or put into a food processor and process to a chunky purée.

4 Return to the pan and add the butter, capers

and remaining parsley. Heat through gently until the butter melts. Adjust the seasoning and turn into a bowl. Serve warm or cold, spread on the slices of crusty bread and sprinkled with chopped parsley.

Seafood Salad

Seafood is plentiful in Italy and varieties of seafood salads are found everywhere.

SERVES 4

175 g/6 oz squid rings, defrosted if frozen
600 ml/1 pint/2½ cups water
150 ml/¼ pint/⅔ cup dry white wine
250 g/8 oz hake or monkfish, cut into cubes
16–20 fresh mussels, scrubbed and beards removed
20 clams in shells, scrubbed, if available
(otherwise use extra mussels)
125–175 g/4–6 oz peeled prawns (shrimp)
3–4 spring onions (scallions) trimmed and sliced (optional)
radicchio and endive (chicory) leaves, to serve
lemon wedges, to garnish

Dressing:
6 tbsp olive oil • 1 tbsp wine vinegar
2 tbsp chopped fresh parsley • 1–2 garlic cloves, crushed
salt and pepper

Garlic mayonnaise:
5 tbsp thick mayonnaise
2–3 tbsp fromage frais or natural yogurt
2 garlic cloves, crushed • 1 tbsp capers
2 tbsp chopped fresh parsley or mixed herbs

1 Poach the squid in the water and wine for 20 minutes or until nearly tender. Add the fish and cook gently for 7–8 minutes or until tender. Strain, reserving the fish. Pour the stock into a clean pan.

2 Bring the fish stock to the boil and add the mussels and clams. Cover the pan and simmer for 5 minutes or until the shells open. Discard any that remain closed. Drain the shellfish and remove from their shells. Put into a bowl

with the cooked fish and add the prawns (shrimp) and spring onions (scallions), if using.

3 For the dressing, whisk together the oil, vinegar, parsley, garlic, salt and plenty of black pepper. Pour over the fish, mixing well. Cover and chill for several hours.

4 Combine all the ingredients for the garlic mayonnaise in a bowl.

5 Arrange small leaves of radicchio and endive on 4 plates and spoon the seafood into the centre. Garnish with lemon wedges and serve with the garlic mayonnaise.

Tortellini

According to legend, tortellini resembles Venus's navel.

SERVES 4

125 g/ 4 oz boned and skinned chicken breast
60 g/ 2 oz Parma ham (prosciutto)
45 g/ 1½ oz cooked spinach, well drained
1 tbsp finely chopped onion • 2 tbsp freshly grated Parmesan
good pinch of ground allspice • 1 egg, beaten • salt and pepper

Pasta dough:
125 g/ 4 oz/ 1 cup strong plain (all-purpose) flour
125 g/ 4 oz/ ⅔ cup fine semolina • 1 tsp salt
2 tbsp olive oil • 2 eggs • 2–3 tbsp hot water

Sauce:
300 ml/ ½ pint/ 1¼ cups single (light) cream
1–2 garlic cloves, crushed
125 g/ 4 oz button mushrooms, sliced thinly
4 tbsp freshly grated Parmesan • 1–2 tbsp chopped parsley

1 Poach the chicken in well-seasoned water until tender, about 10 minutes; drain and chop roughly. When cool put into a food processor with the Parma ham (prosciutto), spinach and onion and process until finely chopped. Stir in the Parmesan, allspice, seasonings and egg.

2 To make the pasta dough, sieve the flour, semolina and salt into a bowl and make a well in the centre. Pour in the oil and add the eggs. Add 1 tablespoon of hot water and work to a dough with your fingertips, adding water if necessary to make it more pliable. Turn the dough on to a floured board and knead it for 10–12 minutes until elastic and smooth.

3 Roll out the pasta dough, half at a time, on a lightly floured surface until as thin as

possible. Cut into 5 cm/ 2 inch rounds using a plain cutter. Place 1/2 teaspoon of the filling in the centre of each dough circle, fold the pieces in half to make a semi-circle and press the edges firmly together. Wrap the semi-circle around your index finger and cross over the two ends, pressing firmly together, curling the dough backwards to make a 'tummy button' shape. Lay the tortellini on a lightly floured tray. Repeat with the rest of the dough, re-rolling the trimmings.

4 Heat a large pan of salted boiling water and add a few tortellini. Bring back to the boil and once they rise to the surface cook for about 5 minutes, giving an occasional stir. Remove with a slotted spoon and drain on paper towels. Keep warm in a dish.

5 To make the sauce, heat the cream with the garlic in a pan and bring to the boil. Simmer for a few minutes. Add the mushrooms, half the Parmesan and salt and pepper to taste, and simmer for 2–3 minutes. Stir in the parsley and pour over the warm tortellini. Sprinkle with the remaining Parmesan and serve at once.

Sicilian Spaghetti

This Sicilian dish originated as a handy way of using up leftover cooked pasta.

SERVES 4

2 aubergines (eggplant), about 650 g/ 1½ lb
150 ml/ ¼ pint/ ⅔ cup olive oil
350 g/ 12 oz finely minced (ground) lean beef
1 onion, chopped • 2 garlic cloves, crushed
2 tbsp tomato purée (paste)
425 g/ 14 oz can of chopped tomatoes
1 tsp Worcestershire sauce
1 tsp chopped fresh oregano or marjoram or ½ tsp dried oregano or marjoram
45 g/ 1½ oz pitted black olives, sliced
1 green, red or yellow (bell) pepper, cored, deseeded and chopped
175 g/ 6 oz spaghetti
125 g/ 4 oz/ 1¾ cups Parmesan, grated • salt and pepper
fresh oregano or parsley, to garnish (optional)

1 Brush a 20 cm/8 inch loose-based round cake tin with oil, place a disc of baking parchment in the base and brush with oil.

2 Trim the aubergines (eggplant) and cut into slanting slices, 5 mm/¼ inch thick. Heat some of the oil in a frying pan (skillet). Fry a few slices at a time until lightly browned, turning once, and adding more oil as necessary. Drain on paper towels.

3 Put the minced (ground) beef, onion and garlic into a pan and cook until browned. Add the tomato purée (paste), tomatoes, Worcestershire sauce, herbs and seasoning. Simmer for 10 minutes, stirring. Add the olives and (bell) pepper and cook for 10 minutes.

4 Bring a large pan of salted water to the boil. Cook the spaghetti for 12–14 minutes until just tender. Drain. Turn the

spaghetti, the meat sauce and Parmesan into a bowl and mix, tossing with two forks.

5 Lay overlapping slices of aubergine (eggplant) evenly over the base of the cake tin and up the sides. Add the spaghetti mixture, pressing it down, and cover with the remaining slices of aubergine (eggplant).

6 Place in a roasting tin (pan) and cook in a preheated oven, 200°C/400°F/Gas Mark 6, for 40 minutes. Leave to stand for 5 minutes then loosen around the edges and invert on to a warmed serving dish, releasing the tin clip. Remove the paper. Sprinkle with herbs before serving, if using. Serve with extra Parmesan, if liked.

Gnocchi Romana

This is a traditional recipe from Piedmont. For a less rich version, omit the eggs. Serve as a starter, or a main meal with a salad.

SERVES 4

750 ml/ 1¼ pints/ 3 cups milk
¼ tsp freshly grated nutmeg
90 g/ 3 oz/ 6 tbsp butter, plus extra for greasing
250 g/ 8 oz/ 1⅓ cups semolina
125 g/ 4 oz/ 1¾ cups Parmesan, grated
2 eggs, beaten • 60 g/ 2 oz/ ¾ cup Gruyère, grated
salt and pepper
basil sprigs, to garnish

1 Bring the milk to the boil, remove from the heat and stir in the salt and pepper, nutmeg and 30 g/1 oz/ 2 tablespoons of butter. Gradually add the semolina, whisking to prevent lumps forming, and return to a low heat. Simmer gently for about 10 minutes, stirring constantly, until very thick. Beat 60 g/2 oz/½ cup of Parmesan into the semolina, followed by the eggs. Continue beating until the mixture is quite smooth.

2 Spread out the semolina mixture in an even layer about 1 cm/½ inch thick on a sheet of baking parchment or in a large oiled baking tin (pan), smoothing the surface with a wet spatula. Leave until cold, then chill for about 1 hour or until firm. Cut the gnocchi into circles about 4 cm/1½ inches in diameter, using a greased plain pastry cutter.

3 Thoroughly grease a shallow ovenproof dish, or 4 individual dishes. Lay the gnocchi trimmings in the base of the dish and cover with overlapping circles of gnocchi. Melt the remaining butter and drizzle all over the gnocchi, then sprinkle first with the remaining Parmesan and then with the Gruyère.

4 Cook the gnocchi in a preheated oven, 200°C/ 400°F/Gas Mark 6, for 25–30 minutes until the top is golden brown. Serve hot, garnished with basil sprigs.

Tomato & Courgette (Zucchini) Frittata

A frittata is a type of Italian omelette thick with a variety of vegetables, fish or meat. You can add almost anything to the eggs. It is also delicious eaten cold (but not chilled) and makes an ideal picnic dish.

SERVES 4

3 tbsp olive oil
1 onion, chopped
2 garlic cloves, chopped
250 g/8 oz courgettes (zucchini), sliced thinly
4 eggs
425 g/14 oz can borlotti beans, drained and rinsed
3 tomatoes, skinned and chopped
2 tbsp chopped fresh parsley
1 tbsp chopped fresh basil
60 g/2 oz/½ cup Gruyère (Swiss) cheese, grated
salt and pepper

1 Heat 2 tablespoons of the oil in a frying pan (skillet) and fry the onion and garlic stirring occasionally, until soft. Add the courgettes (zucchini) and cook until softened.

2 Break the eggs into a bowl and add the salt and pepper, fried vegetables, beans, tomatoes and herbs.

3 Heat the remaining oil in a 24 cm/9½ inch omelette pan, add the egg mixture and fry gently for 5 minutes until the eggs have almost set and the underside is brown.

4 Sprinkle the cheese over the top and place the pan under a preheated moderate grill (broiler) for 3–4 minutes until set on the top but still moist in the middle. Cut into wedges and serve warm or at room temperature.

Polenta

Polenta is prepared in a variety of ways and can be hot or cold, sweet or savoury.

SERVES 4

1.5 litres/2⅓ pints/7 cups water • 1½ tsp salt
300 g/10 oz/2 cups polenta or cornmeal flour
2 beaten eggs (optional)
125 g/4 oz/2 cups fresh fine white breadcrumbs (optional)
vegetable oil, for frying and oiling

Tomato sauce:
2 tbsp olive oil • 1 small onion, chopped
1 garlic clove, chopped
425 g/14 oz can of chopped tomatoes
2 tbsp chopped parsley • 1 tsp dried oregano
2 bay leaves • 2 tbsp tomato purée (paste)
1 tsp sugar • salt and pepper

1 Bring the water and salt to the boil in a large pan and gradually sprinkle in the polenta or cornmeal flour, stirring all the time to prevent lumps forming. Simmer very gently, stirring frequently, until the polenta becomes very thick and starts to draw away from the sides of the pan, about 30–35 minutes. It is likely to splatter, in which case partially cover the pan.

2 Thoroughly oil a shallow tin, about 28 × 18 cm/11 × 7 inches, and spoon in the polenta. Spread out evenly, using a wet spatula. Allow to cool, then leave to stand for a few hours at room temperature, if possible.

3 Cut the polenta into 30–36 squares. Heat the oil in a frying pan (skillet) and fry the pieces until golden brown all over, turning several times – about 5 minutes. Alternatively, dip each piece of polenta in beaten egg and coat in

breadcrumbs before frying in the hot oil.

4 To make the tomato sauce, heat the oil in a pan over a medium heat and fry the onion until soft. Add the garlic and fry for 1 minute. Stir in the chopped tomatoes, parsley, oregano, bay leaves, tomato purée (paste), sugar, salt and pepper. Bring the sauce to the boil, then simmer, uncovered, for 15–20 minutes until it has reduced by half. Adjust the seasoning if necessary. Discard the bay leaves. Serve the polenta with the tomato sauce.

Tagliatelle with Pumpkin

This unusual pasta dish comes from the Emilia Romagna region.

SERVES 4

500 g/1 lb pumpkin or butternut squash
2 tbsp olive oil • 1 onion, chopped finely
2 garlic cloves, crushed • 4–6 tbsp chopped fresh parsley
good pinch of ground or freshly grated nutmeg
about 250 ml/8 fl oz/1 cup chicken or vegetable stock
125 g/4 oz Parma ham (prosciutto), cut into narrow strips
275 g/9 oz tagliatelle, green or white (fresh or dried)
150 ml/¼ pint/⅔ cup double (heavy) cream
salt and pepper • freshly grated Parmesan, to serve

1 Peel the pumpkin or butternut squash and scoop out the seeds and membrane. Cut the flesh into 1 cm/½ inch dice.

2 Heat the oil in a pan and gently fry the onion and garlic until soft. Add half the parsley and fry for 1–2 minutes. Add the squash or pumpkin and continue to cook for 2–3 minutes. Season well with salt, pepper and nutmeg. Add half the stock, bring to the boil, cover and simmer for about 10 minutes or until the pumpkin is tender, adding more stock as necessary. Add the Parma ham (prosciutto) and continue to cook for 2 minutes, stirring frequently.

3 Meanwhile, cook the tagliatelle in a large saucepan of boiling salted water, allowing 3–4 minutes for fresh pasta or 12 minutes for dried (or follow the directions on the packet). When tender but still with some bite, drain thoroughly and turn into a warmed dish.

4 Add the cream to the ham mixture and heat gently until really hot. Adjust the seasoning and spoon over the pasta. Sprinkle with the remaining parsley and the grated Parmesan.

Milanese Risotto

Italian rice is a round, short-grained variety with a nutty flavour, which is essential for a good risotto. Arborio is a good one to use.

SERVES 4

2 good pinches of saffron threads
1 large onion, chopped finely
1–2 garlic cloves, crushed
90 g/3 oz/6 tbsp butter
350 g/12 oz/1⅔ cups Arborio or other short-grain Italian rice
150 ml/¼ pint/⅔ cup dry white wine
1.25 litres/2¼ pints/5 cups boiling stock (chicken, beef or vegetable)
90 g/3 oz/1¼ cups Parmesan, grated
salt and pepper

1 Put the saffron in a small bowl, cover with 3–4 tablespoons of boiling water and leave to soak while cooking the risotto.

2 Fry the onion and garlic in 60 g/2 oz/ 4 tablespoons of the butter until soft but not coloured, then add the rice and continue to cook for a few minutes until all the grains are coated in butter and just beginning to colour. Add the wine to the rice and simmer gently, stirring occasionally until it is all absorbed.

Add the boiling stock a little at a time, about 150 ml/ ¼ pint/⅔ cup, cooking until the liquid is absorbed before adding more, and stirring frequently.

3 When all the stock is absorbed the rice should be tender but not soft. Add the saffron liquid, Parmesan, remaining butter and plenty of seasoning. Simmer for 1–2 minutes until piping hot and thoroughly mixed. Cover the pan and leave to stand for 5 minutes off the heat. Stir and serve at once.

Calabrian Pizza

Traditionally, this pizza has two layers of dough to make it filling. It can also be made as a single pizza, as shown here.

SERVES 4–6

425 g/14 oz/3½ cups plain (all-purpose) flour
½ tsp salt • 1 sachet easy-blend yeast
2 tbsp olive oil
about 275 ml/9 fl oz/generous 1 cup warm water

Filling:
2 tbsp olive oil • 2 garlic cloves, crushed
1 red (bell) pepper, cored, deseeded and sliced
1 yellow (bell) pepper, cored, deseeded and sliced
125 g/4 oz Ricotta
175 g/6 oz jar of sun-dried tomatoes, drained
3 hard-boiled (hard-cooked) eggs, sliced thinly
1 tbsp chopped fresh mixed herbs
125 g/4 oz salami, cut into strips
150–175 g/5–6 oz Mozzarella, grated
a little milk, to glaze • salt and pepper

1 Sift the flour and salt into a bowl and mix in the easy-blend yeast. Add the olive oil and enough warm water to mix to a smooth pliable dough. Knead for 10–15 minutes by hand, or process for 5 minutes in a mixer. Shape the dough into a ball, place in a lightly oiled plastic bag and leave in a warm place for 1–1½ hours.

2 For the filling: heat the oil in a frying pan (skillet) and fry the garlic and (bell) peppers in the oil until soft.

3 Knock back the dough and roll out half to fit the base of a 30 × 25 cm/12 × 10 inch oiled roasting tin (pan). Season and spread with the Ricotta. Cover with the sun-dried tomatoes, eggs, herbs and pepper mixture.

Arrange the salami strips on top and sprinkle with the grated cheese. Roll out the remaining dough and place over the filling, sealing the edges well, or use to make a second pizza. Leave to rise for 1 hour in a warm place – uncovered pizzas take only 30–40 minutes to rise.

4 Prick the double pizza with a fork about 20 times, brush the top with milk and cook in a preheated oven, 180°C/350°F/Gas Mark 4, for 50 minutes or until lightly browned. The uncovered pizza will take 35–40 minutes. Serve hot.

Baked Sea Bass

Sea bass is a delicious white-fleshed fish. Two small fish are succulent grilled (broiled), but a large fish is best baked.

SERVES 4

1.5 kg/3 lb fresh sea bass or
2 × 750 g/1½ lb sea bass, gutted
2–4 sprigs fresh rosemary • ½ lemon, sliced thinly
2 tbsp olive oil

Garlic sauce:
2 tsp coarse sea salt • 2 tsp capers
2 garlic cloves, crushed • 4 tbsp water
2 fresh bay leaves • 1 tsp lemon juice or wine vinegar
2 tbsp olive oil • pepper

To garnish:
bay leaves • lemon wedges

1 Scrape off the scales from the fish and cut off the sharp fins. Make diagonal cuts along both sides. Wash and dry thoroughly. Place a sprig of rosemary in the cavity of each of the smaller fish with half the lemon slices; or two sprigs and all the lemon in the large fish.

2 To grill (broil): place in a foil-lined pan (tin), brush lightly with 1–2 tablespoons of oil and grill (broil) under a moderate heat for about 5 minutes on each side or until cooked through, turning carefully.

3 To bake: place the fish in a foil-lined dish or roasting tin (pan) brushed with oil, and brush the fish with the rest of the oil. Cook in a preheated oven, 190°C/375°F/Gas Mark 5 for about 30 minutes for the small fish or 45–50 minutes for the large fish, until the thickest part of the fish is opaque.

4 For the sauce: crush the salt and capers with the garlic in a pestle and mortar and then gradually work in the water. Alternatively, put the ingredients into a food processor or blender and blend until smooth. Bruise the bay leaves and the remaining sprigs of rosemary and put in a bowl. Add the garlic mixture, lemon juice or vinegar and oil and pound together. Season with pepper.

5 Place the fish on a warmed serving dish and, if liked, carefully remove the skin. Spoon some sauce over the fish and serve the rest separately. Garnish with bay leaves and lemon wedges.

Sardine & Potato Bake

Fresh sardines are now readily available, so this dish from Liguria can be enjoyed by all.

SERVES 4

1 kg/2 lb potatoes
1 kg/2 lb sardines, defrosted if frozen
1 tbsp olive oil, plus extra for oiling • 1 onion, chopped
2–3 garlic cloves, crushed • 2 tbsp chopped fresh parsley
350 g/12 oz ripe tomatoes, peeled and sliced
or 425 g/14 oz can of peeled tomatoes, partly drained and chopped
1–2 tbsp chopped fresh Italian herbs, such as oregano, thyme, rosemary, marjoram
150 ml/¼ pint/⅔ cup dry white wine • salt and pepper

1 Put the potatoes in a pan of salted water, bring to the boil, cover and simmer for 10 minutes then drain. When cool enough to handle, cut into slices about 5 mm/¼ inch thick.

2 Gut and clean the fish, cut off their heads and tails, and slit open the length of the belly. Turn the fish over so the skin is upwards and press firmly along the backbone to loosen the bones. Turn over again and carefully remove the backbone. Wash the fish in cold water, drain well and dry on paper towels.

3 Heat the oil in a pan and fry the onion and garlic until soft, but not coloured. Arrange the potatoes in a well-oiled ovenproof dish and sprinkle with the onions and then the parsley and plenty of seasoning. Lay the open sardines over the potatoes, skin-side down, then cover with the tomatoes and the Italian herbs. Pour on the wine and season again.

4 Cook uncovered in a preheated oven, 190°C/375°F/Gas Mark 5, for about 40 minutes until the fish is tender. If the casserole dries out, add more wine.

Italian Fish Stew

This wonderfully robust stew is full of fine Mediterranean flavours such as basil, lemon and tomato. As you can use any firm white fish, it's ideal for using whatever is most economical.

SERVES 4

2 tbsp olive oil • 2 red onions, finely chopped
1 garlic clove, crushed
2 courgettes (zucchini), sliced
425 g/14 oz can of chopped tomatoes
900 ml/1½ pints/3½ cups fish or vegetable stock
90 g/3 oz dried pasta shapes
350 g/12 oz firm white fish, such as cod, haddock or hake
1 tbsp chopped fresh basil or oregano or 1 tsp dried oregano
1 tsp grated lemon rind
1 tbsp cornflour (cornstarch)
1 tbsp water • salt and pepper
sprigs of fresh basil or oregano, to garnish

1 Heat the oil in a large saucepan and fry the onions and garlic for 5 minutes. Add the courgettes (zucchini) and cook for 2–3 minutes, stirring often. Add the tomatoes and stock to the saucepan and bring to the boil. Add the pasta, cover and reduce the heat. Simmer for 5 minutes.

2 Skin and bone the fish, then cut into chunks. Add to the saucepan with the basil or oregano and lemon rind and cook gently for 5 minutes until the fish is opaque and flakes easily. Take care not to overcook it.

3 Blend the cornflour (cornstarch) with the water and stir into the stew. Cook gently for 2 minutes, stirring, until thickened. Season to taste and ladle into 4 warmed soup bowls. Garnish with basil or oregano sprigs and serve at once.

Trout in Red Wine

This recipe from Trentino is best when the fish are freshly caught, but it gives any trout an interesting flavour.

SERVES 4

4 fresh trout, about 300 g/10 oz each
250 ml/8 fl oz/1 cup red wine vinegar
300 ml/½ pint/1¼ cups red wine
150 ml/¼ pint/⅔ cup water
1 carrot, sliced • 2–4 bay leaves
thinly pared rind of 1 lemon
1 small onion, sliced very thinly • 4 sprigs of fresh parsley
4 sprigs of fresh thyme • 1 tsp black peppercorns
6–8 whole cloves • 90 g/3 oz/6 tbsp butter
1 tbsp chopped fresh mixed herbs • sea salt and pepper

To garnish:
sprigs of herbs • lemon slices

1 Gut the trout but leave the heads on. Dry on paper towels and lay the fish head to tail in a shallow container or baking tin (pan) just large enough to hold them. Bring the wine vinegar to the boil and pour slowly all over the fish. Leave the fish to marinate in the refrigerator for 20 minutes.

2 Put the wine, water, carrot, bay leaves, lemon rind, onion, herbs, peppercorns and cloves into a pan with a good pinch of sea salt and heat gently.

3 Drain the fish thoroughly, discarding the vinegar. Place the fish in a fish kettle or large frying pan (skillet) so they touch. When the wine mixture boils, strain gently over the fish so they are about half covered. Cover the pan and simmer very gently for 15 minutes.

4 Carefully remove the fish from the pan, draining off

as much of the liquid as possible, and arrange on a serving dish. Keep warm.

5 Boil the cooking liquid until reduced to about 4–6 tablespoons. Melt the butter in a small saucepan and strain in the cooking liquor. Adjust the seasoning and spoon over the fish. Sprinkle with chopped mixed herbs and garnish with fresh herbs and lemon slices.

Squid Casserole

Squid is often served fried in Italy, but here it is casseroled with tomatoes and (bell) peppers to give a rich sauce.

SERVES 4

1 kg/2 lb whole squid, cleaned
or 750 g/1½ lb squid rings, defrosted if frozen
3 tbsp olive oil • 1 large onion, sliced thinly
2 garlic cloves, crushed
1 red (bell) pepper, cored, deseeded and sliced
1–2 sprigs fresh rosemary
150 ml/¼ pint/⅔ cup dry white wine and
250 ml/8 fl oz/1 cup water, or
350 ml/12 fl oz/1½ cups water or fish stock
425 g/14 oz can of chopped tomatoes
2 tbsp tomato purée (paste)
1 tsp paprika • salt and pepper
fresh sprigs of rosemary or parsley, to garnish

1 Cut the squid pouch into 1 cm/½ inch slices; cut the tentacles into 5 cm/2 inch lengths. Frozen squid rings should be fully defrosted and well drained.

2 Heat the oil in a flameproof casserole and fry the onion and garlic until soft. Add the squid, increase the heat and cook for about 10 minutes until sealed and beginning to colour lightly. Add the red (bell) pepper, rosemary and wine (if using), and water or stock and bring to the boil. Cover and simmer gently for 45 minutes.

3 Discard the rosemary. Add the tomatoes, tomato purée (paste), seasonings and paprika. Continue to simmer gently for 45–60 minutes, or cover the casserole tightly and cook in the oven, 180°C/350°F/Gas Mark 4, for 45–60 minutes until tender. Give the sauce a good stir, adjust the seasoning and serve hot.

Pizzaiola Steak

The Neapolitan sauce uses the delicious red tomatoes so abundant in that area, but canned ones make an excellent alternative.

SERVES 4

2 x 425 g/14 oz cans peeled tomatoes or
750 g/1½ lb fresh tomatoes
4 tbsp olive oil
2–3 garlic cloves, crushed • 1 onion, chopped finely
1 tbsp tomato purée (paste)
1½ tsp chopped fresh marjoram or oregano or
¾ tsp dried marjoram or oregano
4 thin sirloin or rump steaks • 2 tbsp chopped fresh parsley
1 tsp sugar • salt and pepper
fresh herbs, to garnish (optional)
sauté potatoes, to serve

1 If using canned tomatoes, purée them in a food processor, then sieve (strain) to remove the seeds. If using fresh tomatoes, peel, deseed and chop finely.

2 Heat half the oil in a pan and fry the garlic and onions very gently until soft – about 5 minutes. Add the tomatoes, seasoning, tomato purée (paste) and chopped herbs to the pan. If using fresh tomatoes add 4 tablespoons water, and then simmer very gently for 8–10 minutes, stirring occasionally.

3 Meanwhile, trim the steaks if necessary and season with salt and pepper. Heat the remaining oil in a frying pan and fry the steaks quickly on both sides to seal, then continue until cooked to your liking – 2 minutes for rare, 3–4 minutes for medium, or 5 minutes for well done. Alternatively, cook the steaks under a hot grill (broiler) after brushing lightly with oil.

4 When the sauce has thickened a little, adjust the seasoning and stir in the chopped parsley and sugar.

5 Pour off the excess fat from the pan containing the steaks and add the tomato sauce. Reheat gently and serve at once, with the sauce spooned over and around the steaks. Garnish with fresh herbs, if liked. Sauté potatoes make a good accompaniment with a green vegetable.

Vitello Tonnato

Veal dishes are the speciality of Lombardy, this being one of the more sophisticated. Serve cold with seasonal salads.

SERVES 4

750 g/ 1½ lb boned leg of veal, rolled • 2 bay leaves
10 black peppercorns • 2–3 cloves
½ tsp salt • 2 carrots, sliced
1 onion, sliced • 2 celery stalks, sliced
about 750 ml/ 1¼ pints/ 3 cups stock or water
150 ml/ ¼ pint/ ⅔ cup dry white wine (optional)

Tuna sauce:
90 g/ 3 oz canned tuna fish, well drained
50 g/ 1½ oz can of anchovy fillets, drained
150 ml/ ¼ pint/ ⅔ cup olive oil
2 tsp bottled capers, drained • 2 egg yolks
1 tbsp lemon juice • salt and pepper

To garnish:
lemon wedges • fresh herbs

1 Put the veal in a saucepan with the bay leaves, peppercorns, cloves, salt and vegetables. Add sufficient stock or water and the wine (if using) to barely cover the veal. Bring to the boil, remove any scum from the surface, then cover the pan and simmer gently for about 1 hour or until tender. Leave in the water until cold, then drain thoroughly. If time allows, chill the veal to make it easier to carve.

2 For the tuna sauce: thoroughly mash the tuna with 4 anchovy fillets, 1 tablespoon oil and the capers. Add the egg yolks and press through a sieve (strainer) or purée in a food processor or liquidizer until smooth. Stir in the lemon juice then gradually whisk in the rest of

the oil a few drops at a time until the sauce is smooth and has the consistency of thick cream. Season with salt and pepper to taste.

3 Slice the veal thinly and arrange on a serving platter. Spoon the sauce over the veal, then cover the dish and chill overnight. Before serving, uncover the veal. Decorate with the remaining anchovy fillets and the capers, and garnish with lemon wedges and herbs.

Pot Roasted Leg of Lamb

This dish from the Abruzzi uses a slow cooking method which ensures that the meat absorbs the flavourings and becomes very tender.

SERVES 4

1.75 kg/3½ lb leg of lamb • 3–4 sprigs of fresh rosemary
125 g/4 oz streaky bacon rashers • 4 tbsp olive oil
2–3 garlic cloves, crushed • 2 onions, sliced
2 carrots, sliced • 2 celery stalks, sliced
300 ml/½ pint/1¼ cups dry white wine
1 tbsp tomato purée (paste)
300 ml/½ pint/1¼ cups stock
350 g/12 oz tomatoes, peeled, quartered and deseeded
1 tbsp chopped fresh parsley
1 tbsp chopped fresh oregano or marjoram
salt and pepper • fresh rosemary sprigs, to garnish

1 Wipe the joint of lamb all over, trimming off any excess fat, then season well with salt and pepper, rubbing well in. Lay the sprigs of rosemary over the lamb, cover evenly with the bacon rashers and tie in place with fine string. Heat the oil in a frying pan (skillet) and fry the lamb until browned all over, turning several times – about 10 minutes. Remove from the pan.

2 Transfer the oil from the frying pan (skillet) to a large fireproof casserole and fry the garlic and onion together for 3–4 minutes until just beginning to soften. Add the carrots and celery, and continue to cook for a few minutes longer.

3 Lay the lamb on top of the vegetables and press well to partly submerge. Pour the wine over the lamb, add the tomato purée (paste) and simmer for 3–4 minutes. Add the stock, tomatoes, herbs and seasoning and bring back to the boil for 3–4 minutes.

4 Cover the casserole tightly and cook in a preheated oven, 180°C/350°F/Gas Mark 4, for 2–2½ hours, until very tender.

5 Remove the lamb from the casserole and if liked, remove the bacon and herbs with the string. Keep warm. Strain the juices, skimming off any excess fat, and serve in a jug. Serve the vegetables around the joint or in a serving dish. Garnish with the rosemary.

Saltimbocca

Literally translated saltimbocca means 'jump into the mouth', and this quick, tasty veal dish almost does that.

SERVES 4

4 thin veal escalopes • 8 fresh sage leaves
4 thin slices prosciutto or Parma ham (same size as the veal)
flour, for dredging • 2 tbsp olive oil
30 g/1 oz/2 tbsp butter • 4 tbsp white wine
4 tbsp chicken stock • 4 tbsp Marsala
salt and pepper • fresh sage leaves, to garnish

1 Either leave the escalopes as they are or cut in half. Place the pieces on to a sheet of cling film (plastic wrap) or baking parchment, keeping well apart, and cover with another sheet. Using a meat mallet or rolling pin beat the escalopes gently until at least double in size and very thin.

2 Lightly season the veal with salt and pepper and lay two fresh sage leaves on the larger slices, or one on the smaller slices. Lay the prosciutto slices evenly over the escalopes to cover the sage and fit the size of the veal almost exactly. Secure the prosciutto to the veal with wooden cocktail sticks. If preferred, the large slices can be folded in half first. Dredge lightly with a little flour.

3 Heat the oil and butter in a large frying pan (skillet) and fry the escalopes until golden brown on each side and just cooked through – about 4 minutes for single slices or 5–6 minutes for folded slices. Take care not to overcook. Transfer to a serving dish and keep warm.

4 Add the wine, stock and Marsala to the pan and bring to the boil, stirring well to loosen all the sediment. Boil until reduced by almost half. Adjust the seasoning and pour the liquid over the saltimbocca. Serve at once, garnished with sage leaves.

Chicken with Green Olives

Olives are a popular flavouring for poultry in Apulia, where this recipe originates.

SERVES 4

4 chicken breasts, part boned
30 g/1 oz/2 tbsp butter • 2 tbsp olive oil
1 large onion, chopped finely • 2 garlic cloves, crushed
2 red, yellow or green (bell) peppers, cored, deseeded and cut into large pieces
250 g/8 oz large closed cup mushrooms, sliced or quartered
175 g/6 oz tomatoes, peeled and halved
150 ml/¼ pint/⅔ cup dry white wine
125–175 g/4–6 oz green olives, pitted
4–6 tbsp double (heavy) cream
salt and pepper • chopped flat-leaf parsley, to garnish

1 Season the chicken with salt and pepper. Heat the oil and butter in a frying pan (skillet), add the chicken and fry until browned all over. Remove from the pan. Add the onion and garlic to the pan and fry gently until they start to soften. Add the (bell) peppers to the pan with the mushrooms and cook for 2–3 minutes. Add the tomatoes and plenty of seasoning and then transfer the vegetable mixture to an ovenproof casserole. Place the chicken on the bed of vegetables.

2 Add the wine to the frying pan and bring to the boil. Pour over the chicken and cover. Cook in a preheated oven, 180°C/350°F/Gas Mark 4, for 50 minutes. Add the olives, mix lightly, then pour on the cream. Re-cover the casserole and return to the oven for 10–20 minutes or until the chicken is tender.

3 Adjust the seasoning and serve the chicken breasts, surrounded by the vegetables and sauce, with pasta or new potatoes. Garnish with parsley.

Tiramisu

A favourite Italian dessert flavoured with coffee and Amaretto. You could substitute the Amaretto with brandy or Marsala.

SERVES 4–6

20–24 sponge fingers (lady-fingers), about 150 g/5 oz
2 tbsp cold black coffee • 2 tbsp coffee essence
2 tbsp Amaretto • 4 egg yolks
90 g/3 oz/½ cup caster (superfine) sugar
few drops of vanilla essence • grated rind of ½ lemon
350 g/12 oz Mascarpone cheese (Italian full-fat cream cheese)
2 tsp lemon juice
250 ml/8 fl oz/1 cup double (heavy) cream
1 tbsp milk
30 g/1 oz/⅓ cup flaked (slivered) almonds, lightly toasted
2 tbsp cocoa powder • 1 tbsp icing (confectioners') sugar

1 Arrange almost half the sponge fingers (lady-fingers) in the base of a glass bowl or serving dish. Combine the black coffee, coffee essence and Amaretto and pour just over half of the mixture over the fingers.

2 Put the egg yolks into a heatproof bowl with the sugar, vanilla essence and lemon rind. Stand over a saucepan of gently simmering water and whisk until very thick and creamy and the whisk leaves a very heavy trail when lifted from the bowl.

3 Put the Mascarpone cheese in a bowl with the lemon juice and beat until smooth. Combine the egg and Mascarpone cheese mixtures and when evenly blended pour half over the sponge fingers (lady-fingers) and spread out evenly.

4 Add another layer of fingers, sprinkle with the remaining coffee and Amaretto mixture and then cover with the rest of the cheese mixture. Chill for at least 2 hours, or overnight.

5 To serve, whip the cream and milk together until stiff and spread or pipe over the dessert. Sprinkle with the flaked (slivered) almonds and then sift an even layer of cocoa powder so the top is covered. Finally, sift a light layer of icing (confectioners') sugar over the cocoa.

Zabaglione

Serve this light dessert warm or chilled, accompanied by sponge fingers (lady-fingers) or amaretti biscuits, and soft fruits.

SERVES 4

6 egg yolks
90 g/3 oz/½ cup caster (superfine) sugar
6 tbsp Marsala
strawberries or raspberries (optional)
amaretti biscuits or sponge fingers (lady-fingers) (optional)

1 Put the egg yolks into a heatproof bowl and whisk until a pale yellow colour, using a rotary, balloon or electric whisk.

2 Whisk in the caster (superfine) sugar, followed by the Marsala, continuing to whisk all the time.

3 Stand the bowl over a saucepan of very gently simmering water, or transfer to the top of a double boiler, and continue to whisk until the mixture thickens sufficiently to form soft peaks. On no account allow the water to boil or the zabaglione will over-cook and turn into scrambled eggs. Scrape around the sides of the bowl from time to time while whisking. As soon as the mixture is really thick and foamy, remove from the heat and continue to whisk for a couple of minutes longer.

4 Pour immediately into stemmed glasses and serve warm; or leave until cold and serve chilled.

5 Fruits such as strawberries or raspberries, or crumbled sponge fingers (lady-fingers) or amaretti biscuits may be placed in the base of the glasses before adding the zabaglione.

Panforte di Siena

This famous Tuscan honey and nut cake is a Christmas speciality. In Italy it is sold in pretty boxes, and served in very thin slices.

SERVES 12

125 g/4 oz/¾ cup split whole almonds
125 g/4 oz/1 cup hazelnuts
90 g/3 oz/½ cup cut mixed peel
60 g/2 oz/⅓ cup no-soak dried apricots
60 g/2 oz glacé or crystallized pineapple
grated rind of 1 large orange
60 g/2 oz/⅔ cup plain (all-purpose) flour
2 tbsp cocoa powder • 2 tsp ground cinnamon
125 g/4 oz/½ cup caster (superfine) sugar
175 g/6 oz/¾ cup honey
icing (confectioners') sugar, for dredging

1 Toast the almonds under the grill (broiler) until lightly browned and place in a bowl. Toast the hazelnuts until the skins split. Place on a dry tea towel (dish cloth) and rub off the skins. Roughly chop the hazelnuts and add to the almonds with the mixed peel. Chop the apricots and pineapple finely, add to the nuts with the orange rind and mix well.

2 Sift the flour with the cocoa and cinnamon, add to the nut mixture and mix evenly.

3 Line a round 20 cm/8 inch cake tin or deep loose-based flan tin with baking parchment.

4 Put the sugar and honey into a saucepan and heat until the sugar dissolves, then boil gently for about 5 minutes or until the mixture thickens and begins to turn a deeper shade of brown. Quickly add to the nut mixture and mix evenly. Turn into the prepared tin and level the top using the back of a damp spoon.

5 Cook in a preheated oven, 150°C/300°F/Gas Mark 2, for 1 hour. Remove from the oven and leave in the tin until cold. Remove from the tin and peel off the baking parchment. Before serving, dredge the cake with sifted icing (confectioners') sugar. Serve in thin slices.

Ricotta Ice Cream

Ice cream is a traditional Italian dish, and the numerous flavours available are usually sold in a cone. It is also served sliced.

SERVES 4–6

30 g/1 oz/¼ cup pistachio nuts
30 g/1 oz/¼ cup walnuts or pecan nuts
30 g/1 oz/¼ cup chopped hazelnuts, toasted
grated rind of 1 orange • grated rind of 1 lemon
30 g/1 oz/2 tbsp crystallized or stem ginger
30 g/1 oz/2 tbsp glacé (candied) cherries
30 g/1 oz/¼ cup dried apricots
30 g/1 oz/3 tbsp raisins
500 g/1 lb Ricotta
2 tbsp Maraschino, Amaretto or brandy
1 tsp vanilla essence • 4 egg yolks
125 g/4 oz/⅔ cup caster (superfine) sugar

To decorate:
whipped cream
a few glacé cherries, pistachio nuts or mint leaves

1 Roughly chop the pistachio nuts and walnuts and mix with the toasted hazelnuts, orange and lemon rinds. Finely chop the ginger, cherries, apricots and raisins, and add to the bowl. Stir the Ricotta evenly through the fruit mixture, then beat in the liqueur and vanilla essence.

2 Put the egg yolks and sugar in a bowl and whisk hard until very thick and creamy – they may be whisked over a pan of gently simmering water to speed up the process. Leave to cool if necessary. Carefully fold the Ricotta mixture evenly through the beaten eggs and sugar until smooth.

3 Line a 18 × 12 cm/7 × 5 inch loaf tin (pan) with a double layer of cling

film (plastic wrap) or baking parchment. Pour in the Ricotta mixture, level the top, cover with more cling film (plastic wrap) or baking parchment and chill in the freezer until firm – at least overnight.

4 To serve, remove the ice-cream from the tin (pan) and peel off the cling film or parchment. Place on a serving dish and decorate with whipped cream, glacé (candied) cherries, pistachio nuts or mint leaves.

Index